My Animal Art Class

Nellie Shepherd

A Dorling Kindersley Book

LONDON, NEW YORK, MUNICH, MELBOURNE, AND DELHI

Editor Penny Smith
Designers Melanie Whittington, Jane Horne,
Wendy Bartlet, Lynne Moulding, Victoria Long
Managing Art Editor Diane Thistlethwaite
Production Rochelle Talary
Photography Stephen Hepworth

For Anne Lumb (My Wonderful Auntie!)

ACKNOWLEDGEMENTS
With thanks to: Alex, Alfie, Benjamin, Grace, Haydon, Heather, Helena, Jacob, Jessami, Jessica,
Lauren, Lucy, Max, Melissa, Mikey, Rebecca, Richard, Sam, Sophie, Tom, and Uzair for taking
part in the photographs; Jean Gollner, Anne Lumb, Wendy Morrison, James Pendrich,
Emma Hardy, Melena and Megan Smart (MMKS Logistics), David Hansel
(Memery Crystal), Peggy Atherton, Donna Huddleston, and Gwen Turner.

First published in Great Britain in 2003
by Dorling Kindersley Limited
80 Strand, London WC2R ORL
A Penguin Company
2 4 6 8 10 9 7 5 3 1

A CIP catalogue record
for this book is available
from the British Library

ISBN: 1-4053-0081-7

Colour reproduction by GRB Editrice, Italy
Printed and bound in Italy by L.E.G.O.

See
Dorling Kindersley's
complete catalogue at
www.dk.com

745·592

Where to find things

My Animal Art Class

This book is full of animal characters for you and your children to create together.

Making animals is so exciting! In my art class, they can look even more fantastic than in real life! Flamingos have glittery high heels, hippos wear cool shades, and monkeys are pink, blue, and green! I hope all the animals become your friends and you have a wild time making them! Go for it!

Nellie Shepherd

Read Nellie's tips on page 46 and be inspired!

Basic Kit

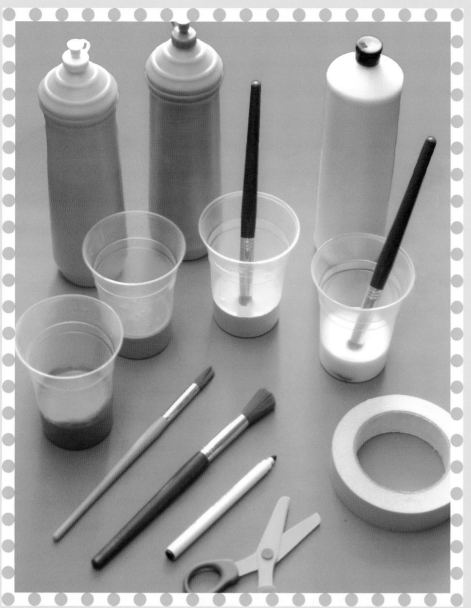

As well as the equipment pictured with each project, you will need the following basic kit:

card	pots (for paint
paper	and glue)
paint	paintbrushes
felt-tip pens	pipe cleaners
PVA glue	play dough
scissors	straws
stapler	fabric
tape (masking	
tape is best)	

Keep your art kit in a box so you can find it easily!

Helping hand

All the projects in this book are designed for young children to make, but they should only be attempted under adult supervision. Extra care should be taken when using sharp equipment, such as scissors, staplers, and pipe cleaners, and with small objects that may cause choking. Only use PVA or other non-toxic, water-soluble glue.

Bingo Flamingo

paper plate

pink fabric

glittery shoes

straws

Making Bingo Flamingo
Is as easy as pie.
You can take her for walks
And she might even fly!

Fab shoes!

6

You can use...

fabric

glitter

glue

card

straws

tissue paper

paper plate

Tot Tip!

We made Bingo using pink fluffy fur fabric, but tissue paper works just as well.

How to make it!

cut

Cut Bingo's shoes, head, and neck from card. Stick scrunched-up tissue paper on the card and all over Bingo's paper-plate body.

tape

Tape Bingo's neck to the back of her body. Tape her straw legs in place and tape her shoes to the ends of her legs.

bunch

For each wing, simply bunch together fabric or tissue paper. Tape the wings in place on Bingo's body.

stick

Stick on card circles for Bingo's eyes. Don't forget to glitter her heels. Now Bingo's ready to play!

Nice eyes!

Kid's talk
"I made my
Blingo with
stickerty stick
fluffy pieces."
Helena, age 3 ½

Debra the Zebra

peg

spoon

plastic cup

I'm Debra the Zebra
All lovely and stripy.
Make me out of cups
And I'm sure you will like me!

You can use...

paint

plastic spoons

glue

pegs

coloured
paper

tissue
Paper

plastic
cups

**Tot
Tip!** Use plenty of tape to hold
Debra together. She will wobble,
but by clipping a peg to her tail
you can make her balance.

Here we go!

tape

Cut the rim off one of the plastic cups and push it inside another to make Debra's body. Tape it in place. You can start to decorate the cups any time you like.

push

Cut four holes in Debra's body, then push a plastic spoon through each hole to make her legs. Push her legs into another cup to make her stand up.

cut

Take another cup and cut out a mouth and eyes (or paint them on later). Cut two ear holes and push two spoons into each. Peg together the spoon handles to make Debra's neck.

Well done!

decorate

Make a hole in the top of Debra's body and push her neck into it. Tape on a spoon tail and clip on a peg to make her balance. Decorate Debra with paper, or paint mixed with glue.

Did you know?
When zebras are in a herd, their stripes make it hard to see where one zebra ends and another begins!

Garth the Giraffe

Hi there! I'm Garth
And I'm a giraffe.
My neck is so long,
It will make you laugh!

cotton bud

chomp
chomp
chomp

pencil

cardboard tube

You can use...

cork

cotton bud

tissue paper

cardboard tube

felt-tip pen

rubber glove

Pencils

Tot Tip! To make funky hooves, snip four fingertips off an old rubber glove. Make a hole in each and put them on Garth.

How to make it!

bend

Bend a cardboard tube to form Garth's head, neck, and body, or cut part-way through a tube and hold it in place with tape. Push in pencils for Garth's legs.

pull

Add Garth's hooves by pulling the rubber-glove fingertips over the ends of his legs.

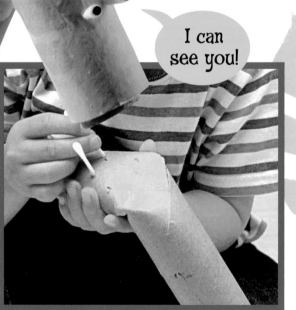

I can see you!

push

Make holes in Garth's head and neck for his eyes, horns, and mane, and push in halved cotton buds. Tape on card ears and add another cotton bud for Garth's tail.

paint

Mix a little glue with paint. Then paint Garth and stick on tissue paper. Stick the cork in place for his nose. Draw on his mouth and eyes with felt-tip pen.

Did you know?
Giraffes are the
tallest animals
on earth!

Tilly the Turtle

I'm Tilly the Turtle.
I swim in the sea.
Make me from sponges.
Then have fun with me!

paper bowl

flat scourer

buttons

Hi!

You can use...

paint

flat scourers

glue

beads

wool

buttons

paper bowl

flat sponges

Tot Tip!

Instead of beads and buttons, you can use dried beans or peas for Tilly's eyes and feet. Simply stick them in place with glue.

Bye!

19

You can do it!

paint

Tilly's the perfect pet! To make her, cut slits in a paper bowl for her head, tail, and legs. Then paint the bowl.

cut

Cut whatever shapes you like from flat scourers or sponges. Stick them on Tilly's back for decoration.

push

Cut out Tilly's head, tail, and legs from flat scourers or sponges. Then push them well into the slits in the bowl.

tape

Glue on buttons and beads for Tilly's eyes and feet. Finally, tape on a long length of wool and take Tilly for a walk!

Whose
pet are
you?

Toothy Shark and Mr Croc

My name is Toothy and I am a shark.
I live in the sea, where it's deep and it's dark.
My crocodile friend has jaws just like me.
They open and close as we gobble our tea!

Snip!
Snap!

Crunch!
Crunch!

Keep away -
we bite!

wooden spoon

wooden fork

You can use...

paint

glue

sand

buttons

wooden fork

wooden spoon

card

Here we go!

 Yum! Yum!

draw

For Toothy or Mr Croc's jaw, draw around a spoon or fork on card. Cut out the shape and tape it in place.

cut

Cut out card fins, teeth, and a tail for Toothy, or card spikes, legs, and a tail for Mr Croc. Stick them in place.

paint

Now paint your animal however you like! If you want to stick things on Toothy or Mr Croc, use paint mixed with a little glue.

sprinkle

We sprinkled our Mr Croc with green sand. Then we glued buttons onto folded card to make sticking-up eyes. We made Toothy's eyes from felt.

play

Let Toothy and Mr Croc play together. Snap! Snip! Snap!

Caterpillar Jo

This creepy-crawly creature
Is colourful and bendy.
She's called Caterpillar Jo
And she's very, very friendly.

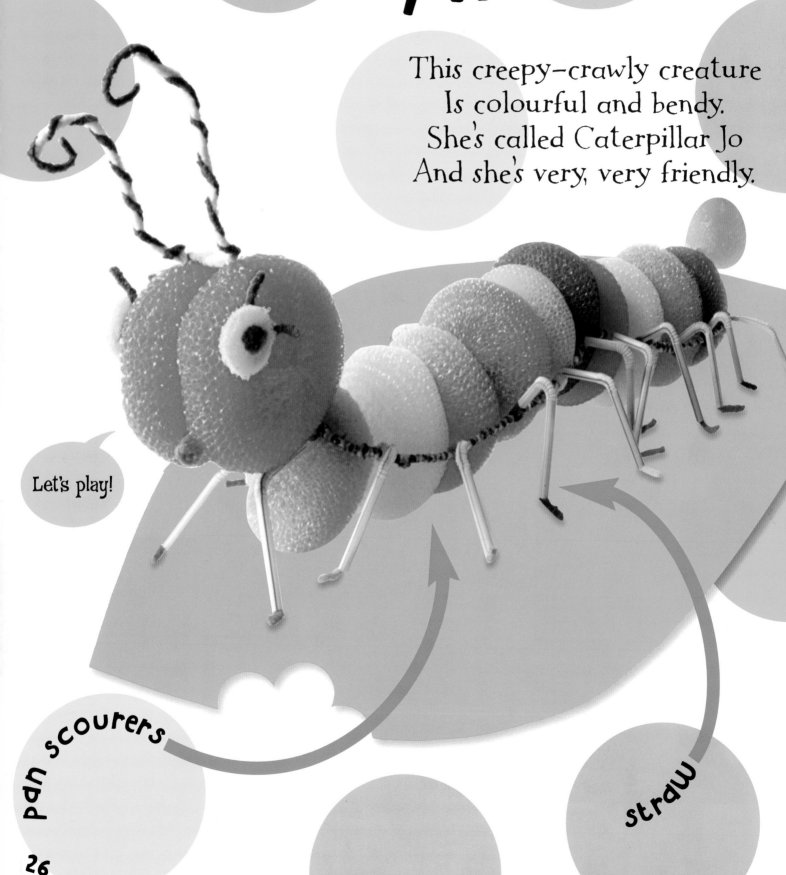

Let's play!

pan scourers

straw

You can use...

pan scourers

pipe cleaners

straws

flat scourers

You can do it!

push

Push pipe cleaners through both sides of a stack of pan scourers to make part of Jo's body. Make two or three sections of body in this way.

join

Join the sections of Jo's body by twisting together the ends of the pipe cleaners.

bend

For the legs, attach pipe cleaners along both sides of Jo's body. Thread shortened straws onto the pipe cleaners. Bend the pipe cleaners to make Jo's feet.

tie together

Use a pipe cleaner to tie together two pan scourers for Jo's head. Push in twisted pipe-cleaner antennae.

cut

Cut out eyes from flat scourers. Push pipe cleaners through the eyes to attach them to Jo's head, and to make eyelashes.

Nice work!

28

29

Horace the Hippo

felt

card

pipe cleaners

Here's a very easy task,
Make this Horace Hippo mask.
Wear it when you want to play
And have a hippy, happy day!

You can use...

card

glue

glitter

paint

pipe cleaners

felt

How to make it!

draw

Draw a large hippo face on card and cut it out. To make a rounded, 3D mask, cut slits in the ears and cheeks (as shown in this picture). Overlap the slits and tape or staple them in place.

staple

For the headband, staple together a strip of card to fit around your head. Staple two card strips to the band to go over the top of your head. Staple your mask to the band.

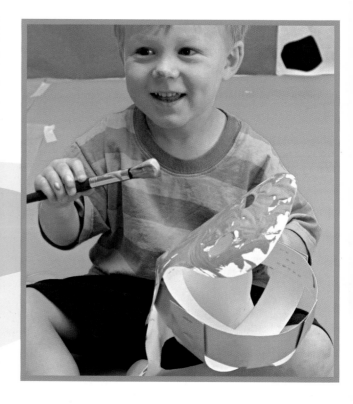

stick

Paint your mask, then stick on felt eyes and ears, and pipe-cleaner glasses. Add glitter, if you want.

Did you know?
A hippopotamus spends most of its day in water. Young hippos swim before they can walk!

Mane Man

I am king of the jungle
And fierce you will agree.
I roar really loud
And I am very proud.
No one dare argue with me!

tissue paper

felt

wool

I'm the Mane Man, king of the jungle!

You can use...

glue

felt

Paint

tissue paper

glitter

wool

card

Tot Tip!

Hold the mask over your face and mark the eyes in the right place before you cut them out.

How to make it!

draw

Draw a lion-shape face on card and cut it out. Paint the face if you like. Cut a nose and mouth from felt and stick them in place. Stick felt or card triangles around the face for a mane. You can stick on felt whiskers, too.

rip

Cut out a long strip of card to make the back of the mane. Rip tissue paper into strips, then glue them on the mane. The more tissue paper you use, the funkier your mane will be!

Be careful here.

roar!

Staple the mane onto your lion mask. Add glitter to your mask if you like. Tape on lengths of wool to secure the mask to your head. Then put it on and roar like a lion!

Did you know?
Only the male lion
has a mane. He lives
in a family group
called a pride.

Monkey Madness

card

We're a group of cheeky monkeys
And we swing high in the trees.
We get up to lots of mischief
And hope that no one sees!

You can use...

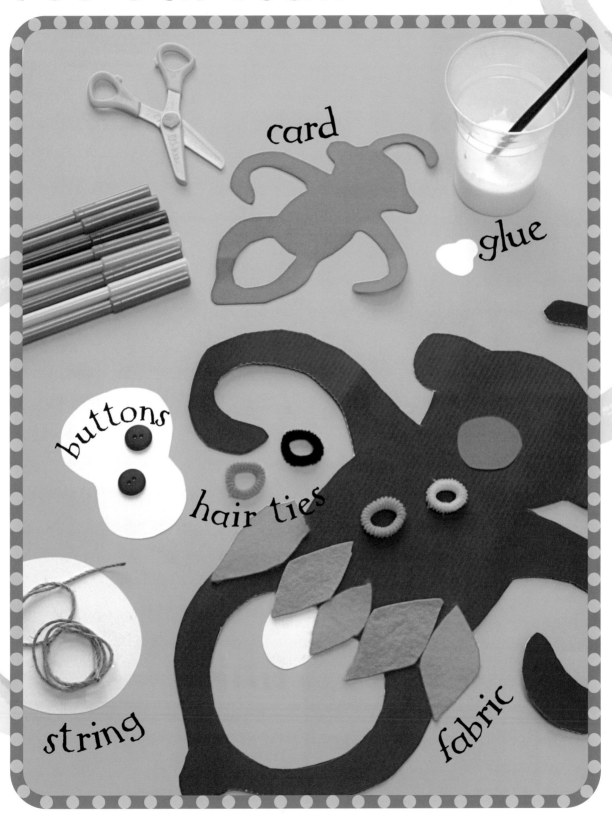

card

glue

buttons

hair ties

string

fabric

You can do it!

Copy me!

copy

Have a go at copying this monkey shape on card. You need one big mama monkey and lots of small baby monkeys. Now cut them out.

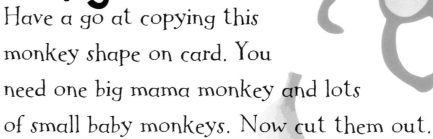

cut

Cut out card shapes for the monkeys' faces, ears, and tummies and glue them in place. Stick on buttons or card for eyes, noses, and mouths, or simply draw them on.

stick

Make clothes for Mama monkey by sticking on fabric leaves and string bows. Thread hair ties onto string for her necklace, and make earrings from hair ties or whatever else you fancy.

link

All the baby monkeys hang from Mama and each other. How many ways can you link them?

40

Did you know?
Most real monkeys have tails. Some monkeys can hang from their tails, keeping their hands free to reach tasty fruit!

Liza the Lizard

I'm Liza the Lizard
All shiny and bright.
Some lizards can change colour,
But I think I'm just right!

Kitchen foil

You can use...

glue

kitchen foil

tissue paper

tissue paper

I'm soooo shiny!

How to make it!

scrunch

Take a long strip of kitchen foil and scrunch one end to make Liza's head. Scrunch the rest of the piece into a long lizard-like body that gets thinner towards the end of the tail.

twist

For Liza's legs, twist two more lengths of kitchen foil and wind them around her body. Add smaller twists of foil for her toes.

wrap

Twist more small strips of kitchen foil to make Liza's curly tongue and sticking-up eyes. Wrap them around her head or glue them on.

glue

To give Liza colour, glue pieces of tissue paper onto her. No two Lizas are the same. What colour is yours?

44

Did you know?
The chameleon
lizard can change
the colour of
its skin!

Nellie's Knowledge

I've been teaching my art class to children for over ten years. Along the way, I've discovered a few tips that make the classes brilliant fun – and help bring out the creativity in all of us!

Organisation
It's good to have all the things you need before you start. But if you haven't got something, just improvise and use something else!

Inspiration
Look at all sorts of bits and bobs. What can you make them into? Challenge yourself and be inspired!

Fun factor!
Think about inviting friends over to join in. Play music and have a story break. It makes such a difference.

Making mess

Art is a messy business! Just put down lots of newspaper, relax, and create. It's worth it!

Encouragement

Encouragement is great for building confidence and creativity: one hundred percent encouragement equals one hundred percent creativity!

Positive attitude

We're positive! In my art classes we never say we can't do something because we simply can!

Making choices

Children's concentration is greatest when they choose the things they want to make. They make their own decisions from the start and they see them through.

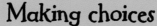

Displaying

Displaying as well as talking about children's art shows it's important. Go on, put it up on the wall!

We've had lots of fun. Goodbye.